Truth Seekers Kids Magazine

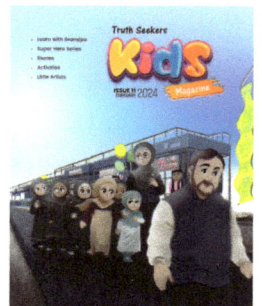

February - 2024 | Issue 11
TS Kids Magazine Team

Mentor
Maulana Syed Abul Qasim Rizvi
& Syed H. Riza

Contributors
By Jafar Hasan,
By Syeda Rabab Zehra,
By Zahra Hasan,
By Fatima Hasan

Designer/Artwork
TS Kids Creative Team

Graphics/Images
TS Kids Creative Team
Mohd. Mehdi

For subscription, advertising, feedback and correspondence please contact:

magazine@tskids.club

 TSKidsClub   TSKidsClub

The views expressed in the Truth Seekers Kids magazine are not necessarily those of the editors or of the Truth Seekers Foundation.

Copyright © 2024 All rights reserved

Disclaimer: All content has been verified by our guide and mentor. Some materials may contain content that is not in full agreement with the religious or spiritual beliefs of other faiths. We do not intend to hurt the sentiments of any individual, community, sect or religion. For reproduction of any content from this magazine in any form, it is necessary to first seek approval from the publisher by emailing us.

From the Editor's Desk

Dear Parents and Young Explorers,

Salamun alaykum,

We are delighted to share with you Issue 11 of TS Kids magazine brimming with captivating stories, inspiring poems, and engaging articles.

In our Superhero story, join Fatima as she embarks on a heroic journey during the Arbaeen walk, showcasing courage and compassion. Uncover valuable lessons about Karbala and Imam Hussain through heartwarming tales with Grandpa, imparting wisdom that transcends generations.

Dive into the enchanting realm of mathematics with fascinating articles that make numbers come alive. Challenge your mind with intriguing puzzles, and let the world of poems take you on a lyrical journey of emotions and creativity.

Our magazine also sheds light on stories of resilience in the face of oppression, offering glimpses into lives that inspire courage and hope. These narratives serve as reminders of the strength within us all.

Exciting changes are on the horizon, and we can't wait to share them with you! Follow us on social media for sneak peeks and updates. As part of this evolution, we have bid farewell to the TS Members Hub account, which is now inactive. Stay tuned for the unveiling of our new features and enhanced content delivery.

Thank you for being a cherished part of our TS Kids family. Your feedback and enthusiasm drive us to create a magical space where learning and imagination thrive.

Warm regards,

TS Editorial Team

Do not be. I am sorry I could not find you sooner. How did you manage to make your way through this crowd and find us?

I am sorry Fatima

That nobleman helped me.

Oh who, and where is he? Well, never mind. I am glad you are back now.

08 | TS Kids | Issue 11, 2024

> We stand before the door of the one so kind,
> Who helped the orphans with an open mind.
> But fate had a test, his own child (Sakina) left behind,
> Salutations to you, O Imam Hussain, your love forever enshrined.
>
> **Labbaik Ya Hussain!**

Aminah and The Rise of Justice

In a distant kingdom, the land of Sakinah was once ruled by a wise and just king named Rashid. The kingdom flourished under his fair leadership, and its people lived in peace. However, as time passed, a new ruler named Amir ascended to power, ushering in an era of oppression.

Amir believed in dominance and control. He imposed heavy taxes on the poor, leaving them struggling to make ends meet, while the wealthy nobles prospered under his favor. The once lively town square became a place of whispers and fear.

In this challenging time, a brave young girl named Amina emerged as a symbol of hope. Amina's family had been severely affected by Amir's policies, and she couldn't stand idly by. With determination in her heart, she rallied the oppressed citizens and formed a secret group dedicated to restoring justice.

Amina and her companions, known as the "Liberators," used their intelligence and courage to outsmart Amir's enforcers. They organized peaceful protests, raising awareness about the unjust conditions in Sakinah. Amina's eloquence and passion inspired people to stand up for their rights.

As the movement gained momentum, Amir grew uneasy. He attempted to suppress the uprising with force, but the Liberators remained steadfast. Amina, fueled by the belief in a fair and equal society, proposed a challenge to Amir: a debate in the town square, where they could present their arguments for the future of Sakinah.

The day of the debate arrived, and the town square buzzed with anticipation. Amina eloquently argued for justice, equality, and compassion, while Amir defended his oppressive policies with arrogance. The people listened, and the atmosphere shifted.

In the end, the citizens of Sakinah realized the importance of unity and justice. They peacefully stood against Amir's rule, demanding a fair government that prioritized the well-being of all. Unable to withstand the united voice of the people, Amir stepped down.

With Amir's departure, a new era began in the kingdom. Amina and the Liberators played a crucial role in rebuilding the land, ensuring that justice and equality prevailed. The tale of Amina and the Liberators became a legend, a reminder that even in the face of oppression, the collective strength of the people can bring about positive change.

Grandpa Series #9

Lessons with Grandpa
Karbala, Love and Imam Hussain

By Syeda Rabab Zehra

"Yusuf, Yusuf!", grandpa called as he struggled to get out of his bed. Yusuf was completely engrossed in a multiplayer game that he was playing over the Internet. Grandpa's weak voice couldn't reach his ears covered with headphones.

Grandpa was sick since a few days. The illness had weakned his body and he required assistance in performing even his routine activities. Jameela just entered Grandpa's room carrying her flowerpot proudly. She was very excited to show Grandpa the little flower bud growing in the plant. 'Look Grandpa, the plant we sow is now blossoming into a beautiful flower', Jameela said excitedly.

'Jameela, my daughter can you please give me some water', Grandpa said as he tried to sit up straight on his bed. "I am so sorry Grandpa, how could I be so ignorant", she replied apologetically after looking at the empty glass and rushed to the kitchen to get some water.

Jameela had taken it as her responsibility to care for Grandpa and attend to all his needs. She knew that her Grandpa is getting old and need more devotion and love.

When she returned, grandpa was gathering all his energy to sit up straight on the bed. 'Let me help you, Grandpa', Jameela rushed to support him sit straight, placing the glass of water on his side table. 'Old age is a difficult period of one's life isn't it, Grandpa?', Jameela sighed as Grandpa settled himself in the soft pile of pillow Jameela had prepared to comfort him.

Jamila handed Grandpa his medicines along with water and sat next to him. She started to share her newly acquired information with her wise and kind grandfather. 'You know grandpa when a person is sick God forgives some of his sins due to the pain and suffering of illness. I read this in a book of ahadith', said Jameela.

'Is that so my dear daughter?' Grandpa asked.

'Yes, grandpa and that's why we should always stay hopeful when we are sick.' Jameela added.

'That's a very interesting information that you have shared with me Jameela', Grandpa replied.

'But you need to take your medicines properly so that you can get well soon, Grandpa. I wonder if you need to change your medicines! You have been taking these medicines since a few days, but not recovered. I think we should consult the doctor again' Jameela said with a concern in her voice.

As always, grandpa wanted her granddaughter to look at matters deeply, not only to what is apparent but to observe and ponder over the the laws of nature and system of God that governs all that manifests in the universe. So, he asked Jamila 'do you believe that the doctor will be able to cure me?'

'Well, that's what doctors are supposed to do, Grandpa, aren't they?', chuckled Jameela.

'My dear daughter there are many signs of God in sickness. Did you observe your Grandpa carefully? Just a few days ago, your grandpa was healthy and able to do all his chores by himself but today you see him struggle to even sit straight on the bed. Suddenly all the power and the energy that he had in his body, and that he used at his own disposition, is not there for him, isn't this something to ponder over? Grandpa asked Jamila.

'Oh grandpa, don't be upset you will be fine. Just keep taking your medicines regularly and you will have your energy back soon', Jameela thought that Grandpa was upset due to his illness and tried to reassure him that he will get well soon.

'So do you believe that the medicines will restore my power and energy, Jameela?', Grandpa presented another question to drive the discussion deeper.

'Grandpa if you take medicines and time and also take care of your diet, you'll be healthy and well soon, don't worry', Jameela replied.

Grandpa wanted to guide his beloved granddaughter to a deeper reality of life, and so he started to ask her a series of questions. 'Have you ever seen people diagnosed with serious illnesses, undergo multiple medical procedures to find a cure for their illness but in the end they die of that illness? Grandpa asked. After thinking for a little while Jamila said, 'yes, I have heard of some people who suffered from chronic diseases or even some people who have cancer and they cannot find a cure for their disease and die of it but how was that relevant here Grandpa?', Jamila asked inquisitively.

'Well, if the doctors can cure us and the medicine can take away our illness and return our health then how come those people cannot find a cure for their illness despite taking all the medicines? Did you ever wonder about that Jameela?'. 'No grandpa, but now that you have asked me, I'm starting to think about this. This is actually interesting because some people will take the same medicine and get well and others do not. If it's the same medicine and the same chemical formula and the same ingredients that we put in someone's body, then how come one person gets well and healthy, and the other person does not. I think that there is something else as well that determines if we get well from our sickness or not isn't it Grandpa?', Jamila asked.

Grandpas was very pleased to see the frowned face of Jameela who had dove into a sea of thoughts hoping that she may be able to harvest a precious pearl of wisdom today. After a little pause Grandpa said 'I do not see any other way of explaining this observation'.

'So, what is it grandpa that decides who gets cured and who does not?', Jameela asked.

'Do you know how medicines are made, my dear child? Grandpa asked.

'Medicines are made from natural ingredients such as plants', Jameela quickly responded.

'Yes, they're made from natural ingredients, but they undergo a long process of testing before they are used and given to people. The testing process is to make sure that a medicine or the combination which is the chemical formula that is made into a medicine works the way it is expected when it is consumed by a person', Grandpa explained.

Jameela who was now getting interested and wanted to show that she is following the discussion added 'so it's a trial and testing process where we extract some ingredients from nature make a specific combination to then target, different diseases in our body hoping that we may find a cure.'

'Correct, if you think deeply about this process, the different medicines that we make are rather a discovery of the natural interactions that have been created by God. What we do is discover how to use them again and again successfully', Grandpa explained further.

Jameela looked a little bit puzzled with this statement.

'But it is still us humans who make those medicines isn't it Grandpa? And if you do not know how to make those combinations that we won't be able to get those medicines right', she said.

'It is true that we discover these combinations, but at the same time we do not have the full control over what happens when someone takes the medicine. For the same reason, many medicines have side effects for our bodies and sometimes are even ineffective. Its similar to this plant', Grandpa pointed to the flowerpot Jameela had brought earlier. 'You know how to take care of this plant, how to protect it from damage, how to fertilise it and help it grow into a healthy tree and give healthy fruit but if I ask you how will you turn this bud into a flower and then a fruit, you would not be able to describe that to me', Grandpa continued. It's the same with medicines, or in fact, anything or any phenomenon in our life. We may initiate the processes and help them sustain but their mechanisms are beyond our control.

'All of these are signs of our God. Yes, a doctor can prescribe me a medicine which will cure my disease, but it is it is God who has given that medicine the properties that needs to fight the disease in my body, and if God has other plans for me then even the medicines won't cure me, my child', Grandpa paused for a while to catch his breath.

Grandpa held up his hand and tried to curl his fingers into a tight fist. 'You see my dear daughter, my hands are shaking. The power that I had a few days ago is not with me anymore'. 'Because you're not the true owner of that power. It is God who has the complete ownership of everything', Jameela exclaimed before Grandpa could finish his sentence.

'And that is why we are told again and again, in the Quran and by the prophets of God that you should always put your trust in Allah. That does not mean that you will not take medicine, but do not be, ignorant of the fact that it is God who has control over the systems of nature, and it is Him who gives cure through medicine and inflict disease. My dear child, I want to rest for a while now'. Grandpa slowly sliced back into hours blanket and closed his eyes shut praying in his heart to Allah to recover him from his illness.

Jameela says thanks to Grandpa for the imparted wisdom and politely left the room. She resumed her position on the couch outside Grandpa's room to keep a check if he needs anything and started to think deeply about agar she has learnt.

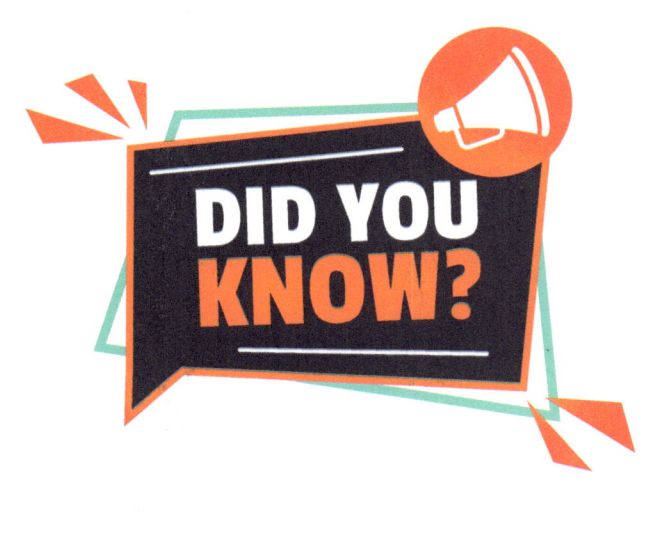

1

Did you know that the Persian scholar of medicine, Ibn Sina (980-1037) suspected that some diseases were spread by microorganisms? To prevent human-to-human contamination, he came up with the method of isolating people for 40 days. He called this method al-Arba'iniya ("the forty").

Traders from Venice heard of his successful method and took this knowledge back to contemporary Italy. They called it "quarantena" ("the forty" in Italian). This is where the word "quarantine" comes from. The origin of the methods currently being used in much of the world to fight pandemics have their origins in the Islamic world."

2

During the Islamic Golden Age, the Persian mathematician and astronomer Al-Khwarizmi introduced the concept of the algorithm, which had a profound impact on the development of mathematics and computation worldwide. His work, "The Compendious Book on Calculation by Completion and Balancing," laid the foundation for modern algebra and revolutionized problem-solving techniques. The term "algorithm" itself is derived from the Latinized version of his name. Al-Khwarizmi's contributions, along with other innovations from the Islamic Golden Age, were influenced by the intellectual and scientific culture encouraged by the Imams, particularly Imam Ja'far al-Sadiq, leading to groundbreaking discoveries and inventions that have shaped the course of human history.

3

The development of the astrolabe: An ancient astronomical instrument used for measuring the position of celestial bodies, determining local time, and navigation. The astrolabe was refined and improved by Islamic scholars like Al-Fazari and Al-Battani, and it played a crucial role in the fields of astronomy, geography, and navigation for centuries.

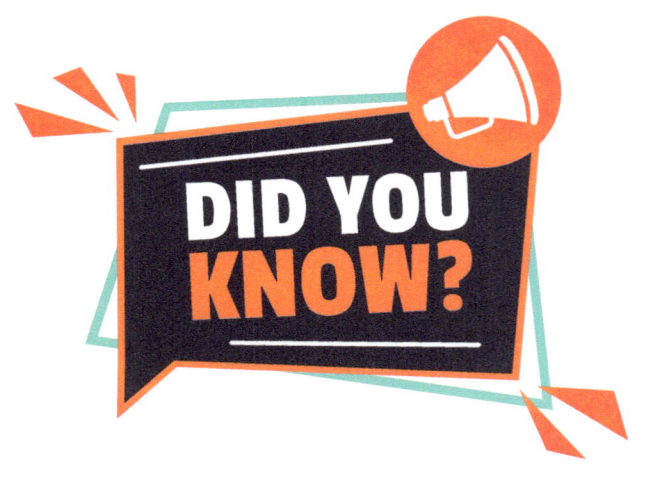

4

Advancements in medicine: The Persian polymath Al-Razi (also known as Rhazes) and the Andalusian physician Ibn Zuhr (Avenzoar) made significant contributions to the field of medicine, including the diagnosis and treatment of diseases, the use of surgical instruments, and the development of medical ethics. Al-Razi's influential medical encyclopedia, "Al-Hawi" (The Comprehensive Book), and Ibn Sina's "Al-Qanun fi al-Tibb" (The Canon of Medicine) were standard medical texts in the Islamic world and Europe for centuries.

5

The development of the crankshaft: The crankshaft, a mechanical component that transforms rotational motion into linear motion, was invented by the Islamic engineer Al-Jazari in the 12th century. His work, "The Book of Knowledge of Ingenious Mechanical Devices," described various machines and automata, including water clocks and water-raising devices. The crankshaft became a fundamental element in the development of various technologies, including the internal combustion engine.

6

The introduction of papermaking: Although paper was first invented in China, it was the Islamic world that helped spread papermaking techniques to the West. Paper mills were established in Baghdad and other Islamic cities, which led to the increased production of books and the dissemination of knowledge. The availability of paper revolutionized the way information was recorded and preserved, ultimately transforming education, communication, and the arts.

These are just a few examples of the many inventions and achievements that arose during the Islamic Golden Age. The intellectual and scientific culture of this era, encouraged by the Imams and other prominent figures, laid the foundation for countless discoveries and innovations that continue to shape the world today

A Tale of Hope in Salaam

In the bustling city of Salaam, little Mustafa and his father Ahmad faced an unforeseen twist of fate when the echoes of a modern conflict reached their doorstep. The initial distant rumblings soon escalated, and explosions rocked their once-secure neighborhood. Tragically, Mustafa lost his mother and sister to the cruel grasp of war. Their once-cozy house, a haven of laughter and warmth, was destroyed in the chaos.

In the frantic moments when their world crumbled, Ahmad, fueled by adrenaline and the desperate need to protect his child, guided him to safety. Amidst the sounds of destruction, he spotted a small, partially intact corner obscured by debris. With Mustafa and the memory of his family in tow, he ran with the speed born of desperation, dodging the falling rubble and seeking refuge in the shadow of the partially standing wall.

Breathless and heart pounding, Ahmad found solace in the lonely sanctuary he had discovered. The distant sounds of war faded into the background as he assessed the meager space that would become their new home. In that moment of respite, amidst the ruins, his determination took root. This corner, though battered and scarred, would be the foundation upon which he would rebuild not only a shelter but a world of wonder for his surviving child.

Determined and creative, Ahmad salvaged remnants of their old life to construct a makeshift house under the shadows of destruction. Discarded furniture pieces were repurposed into decorations, each item carrying memories of their family and the life they once knew. The walls, adorned with colorful drawings and makeshift artwork, became a canvas of imagination. Ahmad turned the scars of war into a magical realm for his son.

To Mustafa, the new dwelling was more than a shelter; it was a fortress that rose from the ruins, a testament to his mother and sister's memory. Ahmad turned mundane tasks into adventures — fetching water became a quest for hidden treasures, and meager meals transformed into feasts fit for royalty. The father and son, once confined by the harsh realities outside, now found solace in the vibrant haven Ahmad had created.

In the evenings, Ahmad and Mustafa escaped the harsh realities of Salaam through a delightful pretend game. Armed with makeshift swords, they embarked on imaginary quests within the confines of their sanctuary. Ahmad, a wise and valiant king, spun tales of ancient lands and mythical creatures, while Mustafa, his trusted knight, embraced the role with a heart full of courage. Navigating through the fantastical landscape painted on the walls, broken glass fragments transformed into magical crystals, guiding them through treacherous paths and secret hideaways. In those moments, the weight of war lifted, and the house under the rubble became a haven of joy and imagination. Ahmad subtly infused each narrative with lessons of hope and perseverance, turning their pretend game into not only a source of entertainment but a means of nurturing Mustafa's spirit. In those enchanted hours, father and son found solace, their bond strengthened by the magic they created together in the midst of war's shadows.

As the war raged on, the bond between Mustafa and Ahmad strengthened within the walls of their makeshift sanctuary. The house under the rubble became a symbol of resilience, a testament to the power of imagination and love in the face of adversity. When the distant sounds of explosions persisted, they would sit together, surrounded by the warmth of their love. In the night, the moonlight cast a gentle glow on the makeshift artwork, turning the once-destroyed space into a sanctuary of hope.

Mustafa, once sheltered from the harshness of war, now found comfort not just in the imaginative tales spun by Ahmad but in the tangible magic he had created amidst the ruins. The house under the rubble became a beacon of creativity, a testament to Ahmad's unwavering determination to protect his child's innocence and provide him with a place where hope could thrive, even in the darkest of times. And in every brushstroke and every salvaged piece, they found echoes of his mother and sister's love, a guiding light in their journey through the shadows of war.

Imam Jafar-al-Sadiq

Imam Ja'far al-Sadiq established a prominent school of learning in Medina during the 8th century CE. His school attracted a large number of students and scholars from various backgrounds and disciplines, and it became a hub of intellectual activity during the Islamic Golden Age. Imam al-Sadiq's school was renowned for its focus on open discussion, debate, and the pursuit of knowledge in both religious and secular subjects.

The teachings of Imam al-Sadiq at his school laid the groundwork for the development of the Ja'fari school of Islamic jurisprudence, which is the primary legal system followed by Twelver Shia Muslims today. His contributions to Islamic jurisprudence were comprehensive and covered a wide range of topics, including rituals, family law, and commercial transactions.

In addition to Islamic law and theology, Imam al-Sadiq's school also fostered the study of various sciences and disciplines, such as mathematics, astronomy, chemistry, and philosophy. Students at his school were encouraged to explore different fields of knowledge, engage in intellectual discourse, and challenge conventional thinking. This open and inclusive approach to learning played a crucial role in shaping the intellectual landscape of the Islamic world.

Notable students of Imam al-Sadiq include:

Jabir ibn Hayyan: A polymath who is considered one of the founding fathers of modern chemistry.
Hisham ibn al-Hakam: A prominent theologian and a key figure in the development of Shia theology.
Abu Hanifa: A renowned Islamic scholar and the founder of the Hanafi school of Sunni Islamic jurisprudence.

The legacy of Imam al-Sadiq's school can still be seen today in the intellectual and spiritual heritage of Shia Islam, as well as the broader Islamic tradition. His teachings continue to inspire Muslims around the world to seek knowledge, engage in critical thinking, and strive for personal and communal growth.

While there are numerous stories and teachings attributed to Imam Ja'far al-Sadiq. They emphasize his intellectual contributions and the wisdom associated with him. One such example is the concept of "al-Muraja'at" in Islamic jurisprudence, which remains useful today.

Al-Muraja'at, or "revisions," is a principle that Imam al-Sadiq emphasized in the field of Islamic jurisprudence (fiqh). It refers to the process of continually reviewing and revising one's understanding of religious rulings and laws in light of new evidence, knowledge, or circumstances. Imam al-Sadiq taught that knowledge is not static, and scholars must constantly reevaluate their understanding to ensure it remains in line with the true spirit of Islam.

The concept of al-Muraja'at is still relevant and useful today, as it promotes flexibility and adaptability in Islamic law. This principle allows scholars to interpret and apply Islamic teachings in ways that address the needs of contemporary society while remaining faithful to the foundational principles of the faith.

Beyond jurisprudence, the emphasis on continuous learning, intellectual humility, and adaptability that Imam al-Sadiq promoted can be applied to various aspects of life, including personal development, education, and professional growth. In this way, his teachings remain useful and relevant even in the modern world.

Mathematica

KNOWLEDGE v/s WEALTH

Hazrat Ali once replied to a group of ten learned men who said, "We seek your permission for putting a question to you."

Hazrat Ali replied, "You are at perfect liberty."

They said, "Of knowledge and wealth, which is better and why. Please give a separate answer to each of us."

Hazrat Ali answered in ten parts:

1 Knowledge is the legacy of the Prophets; wealth is the inheritance of the Pharaohs. Therefore, knowledge is better than wealth.

2 You are to guard your wealth but knowledge guards you. Therefore, knowledge is better.

3 A man of wealth has many enemies, while a man of knowledge has many friends. Hence, knowledge is better.

4 Knowledge is better because it increases with distribution, while wealth decreases by that act.

5 Knowledge is better because a learned man is apt to be generous while a wealthy person is apt to be miserly.

6 Knowledge is better because it cannot be stolen while wealth can be stolen.

7 Knowledge is better because time cannot harm knowledge but wealth rusts in course of time and wears away.

8 Knowledge is better because it is boundless while wealth is limited and you can keep account of it.

9 Knowledge is better because it illuminates the mind while wealth is apt to blacken it.

10 Knowledge is better because it induced the humanity in our Prophet to say to GOD.

"We worship thee as we are your servants," while wealth engendered in Pharaoh and Nimrod the vanity which made them claim God-head

How far is the sun??

A man asked Imam Ali (a.s.) in Masjid-e-Kufa, "What is the distance between me and (pointing towards the sun) and the sun".

It is worth mentioning here about the complexity of this question. This man was an Arab. And in the Arabic language the numbers or count is limited upto one thousand (1000). The count in Arabic does not exceed 1000. The answer to the question this man asked dealt in millions (distance).

It was like a challenge to Imam Ali (a.s.) to answer him in a convincing manner without confusing him.

The man got convinced and walked away.

But it is for us now to ponder on what Imam Ali (a.s.) answered:

"If an Arab horse starts walking from here and continues walking for 500 years, then he (horse) will reach the sun."

The man got convinced and walked away.

But it is for us now to ponder on what Imam Ali (a.s.) said. This one sentence of Imam Ali (a.s.) shows and proves the genius that Imam Ali (a.s.) was.

Imam Ali (a.s.) said "If an Arab horse...", the average speed of an arab horse is 22 mph (miles per hour).

If a horse runs the full day (24hours) it will cover approximately 520 miles. This gives us the distance the horse will cover in 24 hrs (one day).

To calculate the distance covered by the horse in one month we multiply it 520 by 29.5 (Taking an average of the number of months in Urdu calendar. Assuming that 6 months are of 29 days and 6 months are of 30 days.). It gives us something around 15,500. The horse covers 15,500 miles in one month (30 days).

To get the distance that he will travel in one year we multiply it by 12. Since there are 12 months in a year. It gives you 1, 86,000. Then multiply 1, 86,000 by 500 as the horse should run for 500 years. It gives you 9, 34, 00,000 miles.

Now if you ask an astronomer about the distance of sun from the earth he will tell you that the distance is never constant. The orbit of the earth is oval in shape. Sometimes it comes nearer to the sun and on occasions it distances itself from the sun. When the earth is closest to the sun its distance is 9, 10, 00,000 miles and the distance when it is farthest from the sun is 9, 48, 00,000 miles.

When you take an average on these two distances it comes around 9, 30,000 miles.

Imam Ali (a.s.) 1400 years back told us about the distance of the earth from the sun. This also proves that Imam Ali (a.s.) was a genius in Astronomy, Zoology and Arithmetic.

Journey Towards Light

Distance makes everything appear small in sight,

Lost in arrogance, man's perplexed by shortcomings' plight.

Away from the Quran, everything seems trivial too,

With closeness and friendship, guidance's light shines through.

In unity and love, we find strength to prevail,

Overcoming our flaws, with faith we set sail.

Embracing the wisdom, the divine words impart,

Nurtures the soul, and enlightens the heart.

In the pursuit of truth, let us walk hand in hand,

Together, we journey towards a better land.

Note: This poem emphasizes the importance of closeness to the Quran, unity, love, faith, and the pursuit of truth in guiding us towards enlightenment and a better life

Islamic Calendar

The Islamic year has begun anew,
A time to renew our faith and pursue
The blessings of Allah, the Merciful and True.

The Hijri calendar, with its lunar phase,
Reminds us of the Prophet's blessed days,
And the triumphs of Islam in so many ways.

From Muharram, the month of mourning and grief,
To Ramadan, the month of fasting and relief,
We strive to draw closer to our Creator's belief.

Through Dhul-Hijjah, the month of pilgrimage and sacrifice,
We learn the value of humility and compromise,
And the importance of living a life that's wise.

With the Hijri calendar, we journey through time,
Reflecting on our past, and our future divine,
As we seek to please Allah, with every act and rhyme.

So let us cherish this Islamic year,
With its reminders of faith, hope, and fear,
And strive to be better, year after year.

Puzzle

```
M E C C A E A J D R
U H M A D A M A R G
S L I M A K A B A H
L A H A Z A K A T H
I N A B A R A K A T
M A H A M M A D A I
A R T S A F I R A M
R A M A D A N O O A
A Q S A Q U R A N S
Q S A L A T U O M M
I B A D A H A J J E
H I J A B L E A R N
```

Words to find:

ALLAH • MUHAMMAD • QURAN • SALAT • RAMADAN • ZAKAT
HAJJ • UMRAH • ISLAM • MUSLIM • HIJAB • MECCA • MADINA
KABA • AL-AQSA • JUMMAH • IBADAH • BARAKAT

The Honest Trader

Title: The Honest Trader and His Taqwa

Once upon a time, there was a successful trader named Ahmed. Ahmed was not just any ordinary trader - he was a person of Taqwa. He always made sure to conduct his business dealings with honesty, integrity, and fairness, because he knew that these were the values that Allah (SWT) had commanded him to uphold.

One day, Ahmed received a shipment of goods from a supplier, and as he was unpacking the crates, he noticed that one of the crates had an extra item that he hadn't ordered. His first instinct was to keep the extra item and sell it for a profit, but his Taqwa and good moral values urged him to do the right thing.

Ahmed knew that taking something that did not belong to him was against the teachings of Islam. He remembered the Hadith of Prophet Muhammad (PBUH) that said, "The faithful in their love for each other, mercy towards each other and kindness towards each other are like one body; when one part is hurting, the rest of the body responds with sleeplessness and fever."

So, he contacted his supplier and informed him of the mistake. The supplier was surprised by Ahmed's honesty and thanked him for his integrity. He then asked Ahmed to return the extra item to him, but Ahmed refused, saying, "I have no right to keep something that doesn't belong to me. Please take it back and use it for a good purpose."

The supplier was impressed by Ahmed's Taqwa and integrity, and he rewarded him with a significant discount on his next order. News of Ahmed's honesty soon spread, and his reputation as an honest and trustworthy trader grew even stronger.

Ahmed's Taqwa had helped him to resist the temptation of greed and choose the path of righteousness. His actions inspired others to follow the same path and uphold the values of Islam in their business dealings.

Who was this lady?

By Zahra Hasan

They would shout and torture,
But they cannot quiet her.
They would threaten and scream,
But they would not silence her.

Her voice echoed throughout,
Reaching everyone's ears.
A magnificent and royal style,
And yet people cannot recognise her.

She was such an eloquent speaker,
That people thought of Ali ibn Abu Talib.
In Kufa, in Shaam, in markets and courts,
She spread the truth that people could not see.

But who was this lady?
Without a chadar and in shackles,
With other ladies without their chadars,
And one unwell man surrounded by heads on spears.

Her sermon reminded people of Ali,
Her piety reminded people of Fatima,
Her courage reminded people of Hasnain & Abbas,
And her knowledge reminded people of Rasulallah.

She spoke against the oppressors,
And reminded people of their negligence.
She reminded them of what the prophet had said,
About his Ahlul Bayt and Haqq.

Then who was this lady?
Who made the people realise what they had done.

She was the granddaughter of prophet Muhammad,
The daughter of Ali & Fatima.
She was the sister of Hasan & Hussain,
The sister of Kulthoom & Abbas.

She was the mother of Aun & Muhammad,
The aunt of Qasim, Asghar, Akbar, Sajjad and Sakina.
She was the knower of the Quran,
And the first Zakira of Karbala.

She was loyal & courageous,
Eloquent & knowledgeable.
She is Zainab e Kubra,
The brave, lioness daughter, Zainab.

Sadness Arrives

By Fatima Hasan

I gaze at the banner,
As black as it can be.
Staring at the Farsh e Aza,
As sorrowful as it can be.
Wiping my tears as they roll down my cheeks,
I cannot halt them, but with a sigh.
Just the name of Imam Hussain (a.s) makes me weep,
And the masaibs cause agony at its peak.
Sometimes, I ponder, even after 1400 years,
Do we truly connect with their emotions?
Have we comprehended the reasons for his sacrifices and sufferings?
He gave everything in the name of Allah,
To make us grasp the importance of Allah's religion.
I often wonder why Imam Zaini Abedin could never smile.
He witnessed not only Karbala but also Kufa and Shaam.
Reflecting on it compels me to say… Labbaik ya Imam! Labbaik ya Imam!

Little Contributors

What we need

Peace, we need

Armistice, please

Liberate people from misery

Extend hand of peace

Sufferings must cease

Torture needs an end

Injuries should heal

Nonstop war needs to stop

End genocide!

By **Hasan Haider, age 10**

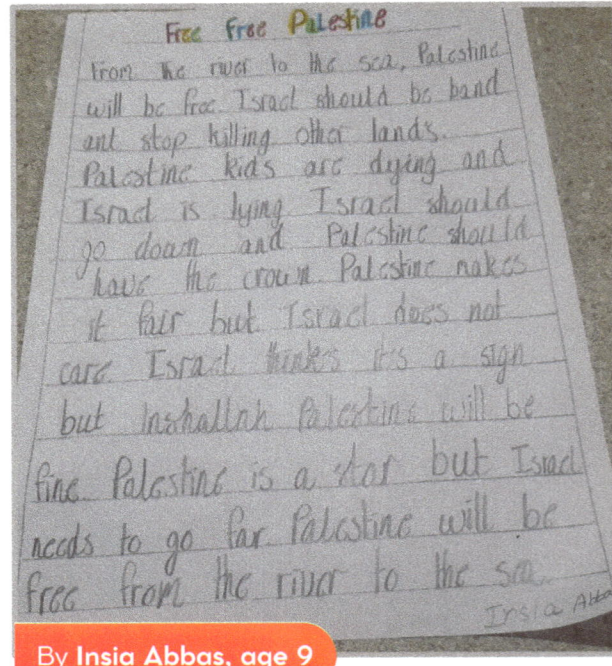

By **Insia Abbas, age 9**

SUBMIT YOUR WORK

Hey kids! Would you like to submit your poem, writing or drawing?

Send it to us by email at **magazine@tskids.club**

www.ingramcontent.com/pod-product-compliance
Lightning Source LLC
Chambersburg PA
CBHW061803290426
44109CB00030B/2926